The Color of Peace

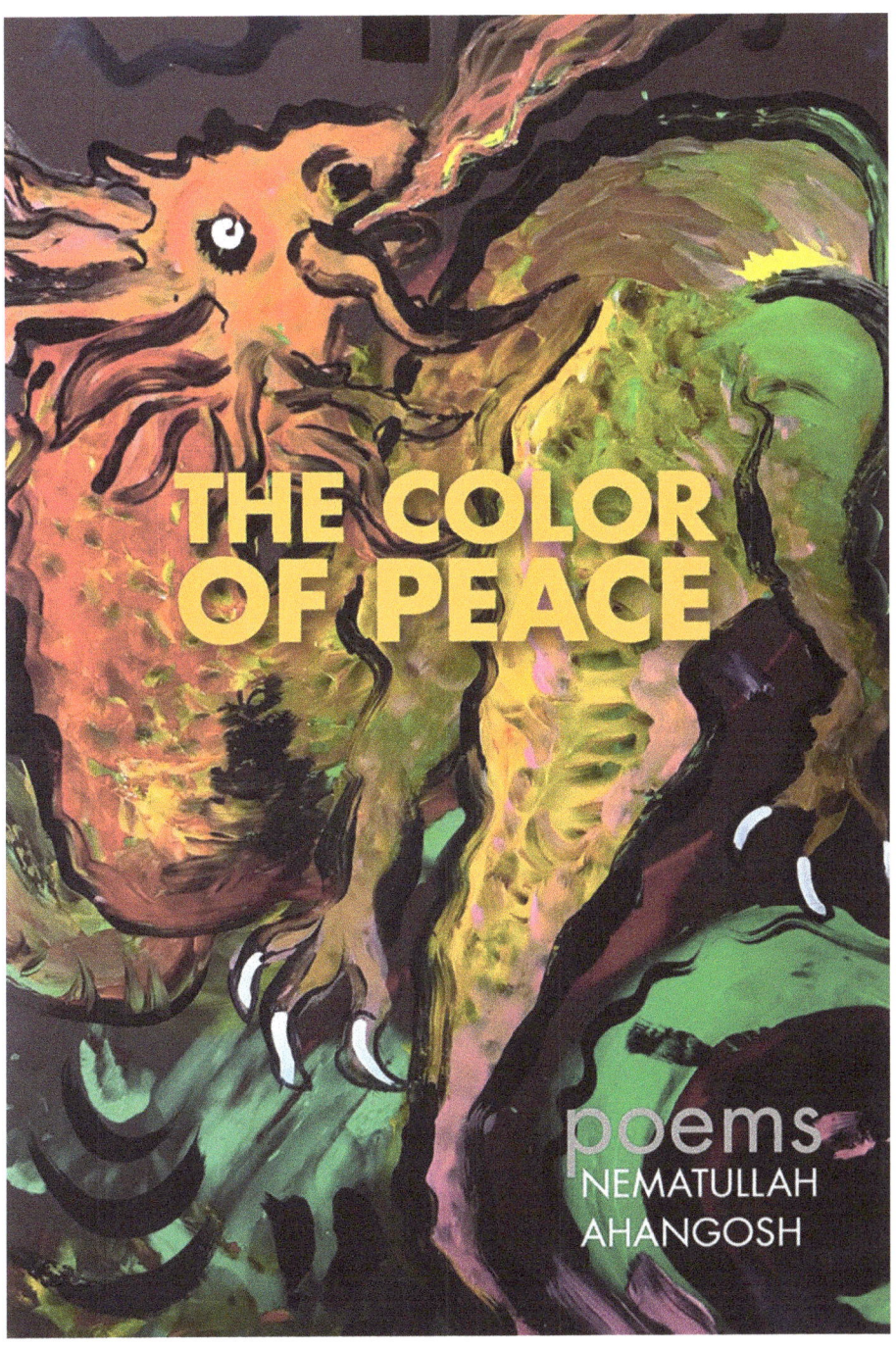

Haley's
Athol, Massachusetts

© 2025 by Nematullah Ahangosh
All rights reserved. With the exception of short excerpts in a review or critical article, no part of this book may be re-produced by any means, including information storage and retrieval or photocopying equipment, without written permission of the publisher, Haley's.

Haley's
488 South Main Street
Athol, MA 01331
marcia2gagliardi@gmail.com • 978.249.9400

Haley's thanks David Smith-Ferri, consulting editor and himself a poet, for his insight and dedication to production of the poetry of Nematullah Ahangosh in *The Color of Peace.*

Haley's thanks Theresa Whitehill of Colored Horse Studios for her design of the cover for *The Color of Peace.*

Copy edited by Mary-Ann DeVita Palmieri.

Cover painting by Steffi Hekli.

International Standard Book Number, trade paperback:
    978-1-956055-25-2
International Standard Book Number, eBook:
    978-1-956055-26-9

Library of Congress Control Number:
    2025933234

for Bakhtawar Ahmadi,
who has nurtured me with love and care

for the women of Afghanistan, especially my sisters—
your strength and love inspire me every day

Contents

The Story Does Not End Here 1
Scaring a Dead Man 3
Fitting In 5
Love in the Time of COVID-19 7
2001 8
Crows? Or Drones? 11
The Cold Refuge 13
The World through Maryam's Eyes 15
At the Edge of Suicide 17
Mornings in Kabul 19
Death Must Be So Beautiful 20
The Reality 23
Teach to Love 25
How We Fight COVID-19 in Afghanistan 26
The Drone and the Butterfly 28
Missing Home 31
One More Time 32
Afghan Peace Volunteers and the Invaders 34
Mother of All Bombs 36
The Question 39
Davis with Visions 40
Grounded and Groundless 43
Traveler and Companion 44
Next Time on Earth 45
The Childish Me 46
Eight Hours 47
What Price Did Abdul Samad Amiri Pay? 48
Hope in the Dark Night 50
Gods Must Have Cursed Earth 52
Our Atomic Life 53

continued

Either We Are All Terrorists or No One Is 54
Dance or Weapon? 56
Colorless Peace..58
Hakim..60
A Question of Questions.....................................62
September in Trance...63
Acknowledgments...67
About the Author 69
Colophon 71

Nematullah's Gifts

a foreword by Kathy Kelly

When I met Nematullah Ahangosh in 2016, he volunteered with an idealistic group of Afghan youngsters eager to abolish war, overcome ethnic differences, share resources equitably, and care for Afghanistan's battered environment. Since the Taliban takeover of Afghanistan, the group has disbanded and, for security purposes, asks not to be identified in writing.

I found it easy to befriend Nematullah, in part because he spoke English so well. I soon learned that he loved to read stories and poems in English. Shortly after we met, he asked me a small favor. Upon return to Afghanistan, could I bring him a book by Alice Munro? He also began sharing with me some of his own stories and poems written in English. Of his coping with an achingly difficult bodily change. His steadily weakening muscles caused him a waddling gait. At times, others mocked him, and even his own family was bewildered by what was happening to him. Doctors in India later diagnosed the condition as muscular dystrophy.

Many of the poems in *The Color of Peace* show remarkable empathy for people who experience pain, grief, and loss. A human rights commissioner is tortured and murdered; attackers kill mothers, children and hospital staff at a maternity hospital in Kabul; weaponized drones rain down missiles on civilian homes.

In "The World Through Maryam's Eyes," Nematullah describes a young girl who loves her school. She loves learning, loves her teachers, and dreams of becoming a teacher. One day, she watches as a bomb explodes, destroying her school. Nematullah passionately wants his readers to understand Maryam's trauma:

> See the terror in her eyes?
> She is terrified.
> All she can see is smoke.
> She sees no friends and no teacher.

No more school, she thinks.
All she can hear is an ambulance siren and guns firing.
The school stands *burning* in front of her.
Her school was bombed in front of her eyes,

I'm particularly drawn to that poem because of having met Maryam.

Nematullah invited me several times to accompany him to a refugee camp where he volunteered with Jesuit Refugee Services to teach math and languages to children of primary school age. I should mention the conditions that prevail in Kabul's refugee camps. Decades of war have displaced millions of Afghans. Internally displaced refugees who crowd into makeshift so-called camps face life-threatening shortages of food, clean water, fuel, and adequate shelter. It's hard for me to imagine harsher circumstances in which to eke out a living.

Nematullah's classroom could, I think, be best described as an oasis within the camp. I watched little girls glowing, simply beaming with happiness as they sat, shoulder to shoulder, on the mud floor of a room with bare walls, learning from their beloved teacher. Nematullah invited Maryam to address my friend Sarah and me because she was becoming so proficient in English. The entire class seemed to share in Maryam's pride and dignity as she stood to welcome us and introduce herself.

It wasn't until I read Nematullah's poem that I learned more of Maryam's story.

The first poem in *The Color of Peace* carries the title "The Story Does Not End Here." The title serves as a theme throughout all of Nematullah's stories and poems. His poetry recounts unfolding events, ideas, and relationships.

I think it's important for readers to know that Nematullah eventually received a scholarship to study at a social work college in India. He completed his studies and then joined an institute in Kerala, India, that supports people in creating an organization to help them realize a vision or dream that impassions them.

Nematullah had been nurturing a dream for many years of being able to assist and train people with fates similar to his—disabled people so they can survive wars and natural disasters. The group he founded is called Stretch More.

A few days ago, I learned that Nematullah had focused on giving swimming lessons to three blind people. Nematullah, who had recently learned to swim, swam every day in the Velliyani Lake while he lived in India. He said it strengthened him and built his confidence.

I'm glad to know he named his new group Stretch More. In an entirely positive way, his writing stretches the truth, not by altering it, but by opening a window for others to understand and embrace the stories he tells and questions he raises.

Not every poem in *The Color of Peace* raises a lament. "Davis with Visions" describes a wonderful friendship Nematullah formed with Davis, a fellow University student. With a hint of fun-filled rebellion, Nematullah describes the two of them getting high together, but the experience evolves into a connection with spirits from former generations.

> In hallucination, figures of our ancestors appeared
> grateful for our friendship,
> we who appreciated our existence,
> our indigo auras coupling us with the old souls.

Stretching beyond limitations, Nematullah's poems reward us with an invitation to see events from his perspective. He helps us see the evil of war as we still treasure our potential for goodness.

Each poem is a gift.

American peace activist, pacifist, and author Kathy Kelly numbers among founding members of Voices in the Wilderness. Until the campaign closed in 2020, she served as co-coordinator of Voices for Creative Nonviolence. She has traveled to Afghanistan several times on behalf of peace initiatives.

The Story Does Not End Here

In the west of Kabul city,
you find a maternity hospital.
Some men armed to teeth
entered the hospital, viciously
killed and destroyed everyone and everything they could see.

Some women were delivering babies in agony.
Some were children born newly.
Some were caregivers of the maternity.
Some were there for humanity,
like Médicins Sans Frontières.
That day they were meant to be slaughtered
by the men equipped with weaponry.

A person tried to call the police
while a bullet made a hiss.
He fell on the ground and rested in peace.
Another tried to escape, but
a brute appeared and
stabbed him in the neck.
A child ran to take refuge
while a bullet passed through his head.
He struggled to survive, but life had refused him.
A visitor made himself a shield, but
he could not fight a grenade that was due.
In a second their skin was floating like butterflies in air.
An attendant hugged a pregnant woman to protect, yet
nothing could help.
Piercing three of them like a net, a spray of nine millimeter bullets
had left the muzzle.

Police and special forces approached with tanks and arms.
They opened fire on the savages.
For a while, police and savages exchanged hot and piercing bullets
until the beasts had no more ammunition.
They succumbed. Some were killed, some arrested,
wounded women and babies rescued.

The story does not end here.
The newborns relocated to a safe place
from where they disappeared into nothingness,
the mothers waiting for their newborns at home,
not aware they were stolen by barons.

What hurts the most is that
Médicins Sans Frontières never returned to rebuild.

Scaring a Dead Man

The women were pacing in peace,
big smiles on their faces.
Their distant laughter faded
as they headed to unknown paths.
I asked, *O, sisters, pray for me,*
yet they didn't hear.

The men came marching,
big bodies carrying their heads,
long hands hanging from shoulders,
big steps speeding up.
I asked, *O, brothers, pray for me.*
They didn't hear.

I saw a woman crying.
Her face was familiar.
She looked old. She was my mother.
A child accompanying her was my sister.
I asked her not to cry! But
she didn't hear.
She was busy collecting my pieces,
crying when collecting.
I realized I was dead a while ago.
As I touched my body, it was cold and relaxed.
After she collected me, I was not a piece but pieces.
I was blown up an hour ago.
Those were my parts.

Women and men gathered
to wash me and connect my pieces.
And they put me in a coffin,

carried me to the cemetery,
cried, prayed as they buried me.
I saw soldiers with rifles.
I asked them not to fire.
They did not hear me.
That is how they celebrated my death,
firing up to the sky,
scaring birds and animals,
scaring a dead man.
My beloved mother, this was my story!
I went to earn a living, and I am sorry.

Fitting In

Sometimes the world becomes so small you can't fit in.
The sun sets, and the night falls.
Unless you have no pain, you don't notice it.
Sometimes you become so small the universe can't fit inside you.
The sparrows on your street perish.
Unless you don't feel pain, you don't have it.
Often you can't face the truth.
You ignore it like puff from a cigar
so bitter you can't swallow.
Look up—sky lies open,
stars wink.
They are us,
like coming home.
Let's cherish their beauty!

Look around. Find us,
how distant we stand.
We are the children
not of Heaven
but of Mother Earth.
Why so much hatred
while we are a family?
Why miles apart?
Why separate?
Why fear love?
Our feelings are the same.
We, too, want freedom.
Do you fear my religion?
I hope that isn't the reason.
Let's praise redemption.

Water Lily
oil pastel on paper
copyright by Steffi Hekli/world

Love in the Time of COVID-19

In the time of COVID-19, you can't turn the clock back.
In such times, you just question the world wordlessly.
In quarantine, no one cares,
especially if your legs don't function as they should.
Who could understand me?
Helpless, I could not protest.
How could you protest
if you were poor,
if you were from war-torn lands?

How could you protest
if people could but would not hear you,
if they could but would not love you,
and, divorced from reality,
most of all, how could you protest
if you were born disabled?

What a terrible mistake my birth must have been,
lacking love from the scratch.

In times like these, I am left all alone
but not lonely, as the stars are with me.

Times like these are an opportunity to learn
that when love enters through a door,
hatred should escape from a window.
In times like these, I open my heart to love
and fill my soul with love.

I am ready for love to enter
and chase the hatred away.

2001

The sky was crying.
Birds were mourning
for the children running everywhere
yet not reaching anywhere
and helter-skelter scattering like flocks of sheep
as if they were being chased by some kind of flying wolves.

You could see jet fighters
swinging like crows and devouring like wolves—
roaring as giant flying beasts
dropping bombs.

A child who was lost was looking for his family.
When he saw his mother, he ran to her.
Both were happy and running towards each other.
A bomb rushed in and connected both to the same destiny
and sent them to the invisible world.

It was 7 October 2001
when they violated my country's airspace,
lacking permission from us and the world.
It was 2001 when they labeled me a terrorist
and their media fed the world with misinformation.

I trust my mother who tells me I am not a terrorist,
who tells me the story of bravery of my father—fighting for freedom.
I can't trust BBC who tells me I am an extremist.
I don't trust VOA who tells me I am a terrorist.
I trust my sister who calls me a nerd.
Finally, yet importantly, I trust myself.

I am aware the world used my sacred country,
made it a safe haven for those who fight one another,
but I am not a fighter
nor will I stand with any side
but the truth,
and that truth is me.

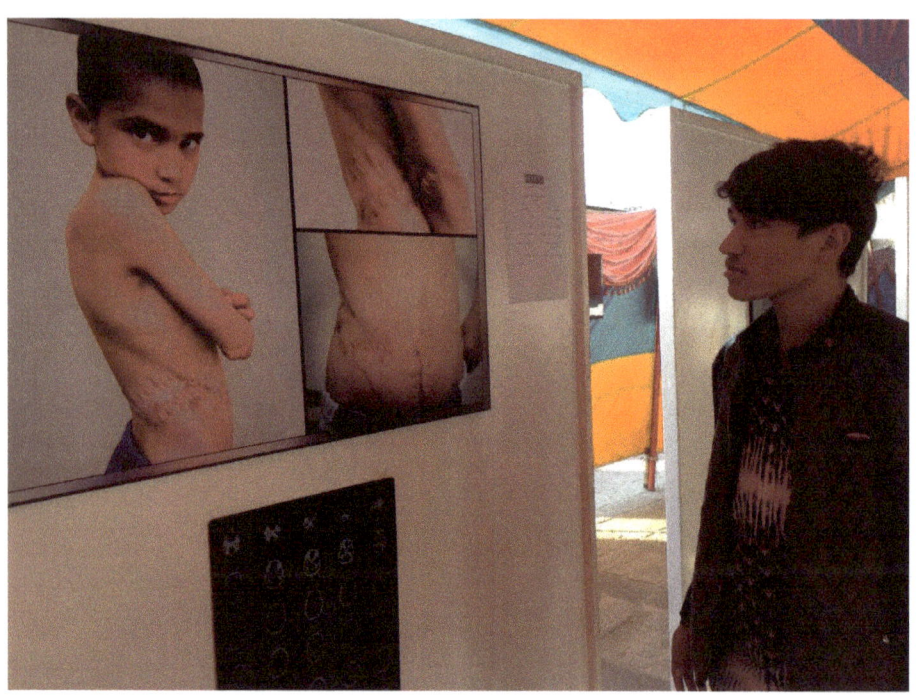

Nemat at Scars of War Exhibition, Kabul
photograph copyright by Davis Panna

Crows? Or Drones?

I dreamed I could be infinitely happy.
I was told that birds can fly
to the whereabouts of the infinite cosmos,
travel the furthest of the far
in an astral trip to the ocean of stars,
that the sun created rainbows within every dew drop.

Now I see we can't protect ourselves from one another,
and I see not only birds in the sky
but drones that fly higher and faster.
They shower us with bullets
and create infinite darkness
and roar louder than the rumble of thunder.

Once a bomb, dropped by a drone, fell on a house.
It killed infants and women and old.
You could see flocks of the crows landing on bodies
as if the drone gave a party for the crows.

The folks gathered and wept
and cursed the drone and the crows,
but all disappeared long ago.
They doubted who to blame.
Drones that killed them by bomb flames?
Or crows who left nothing but frames?
The one who kills or the ones who dine?

The Cold Refuge
acrylic, permanent marker, and touch-up pen on coated cardboard
copyright by Steffi Hekli/world

The Cold Refuge

The young and old couples entered our refuge.
Every young kid who saw them stood excited.
The couples brought clothes and food.
They glanced at me whenever they could,
hoping I would welcome them like others would.

They carried fancy DSLRs
and were always after smiles
in order to capture and send them to the so-called world.
They promised the world would hear our voice.
At the time, we did not realize
that they were after photography prizes.
Learning about it for us was a surprise.
Gradually, their visits became concise.
They never understood our cold refuge
and how we waited in the cold mornings for the sunrise
because the clothes they brought did not suffice,
and most of them were not our size.

The Third World is where the photographers make money.
How poor the First World and Second World are,
and how simple minded the Third World is.
How stupid we all are
that we see who took the picture
and not those in the picture.

School Girls in Bamiyan
photograph copyright by Hakim Young

The World through Maryam's Eyes

Maryam walks to school every morning
to get a little from the stream of knowledge,
and she loves her school.
Every morning, she greets her friends.
The school is far from her home,
and she loves her school.

Maryam is a young girl
who just learned arithmetic,
and she loves her teachers
who taught her the alphabet.
She dreams to be a teacher one day.

Today she stands staring motionless
in front of her school.
See the terror in her eyes?
She is terrified.
All she can see is smoke.
She sees no friends and no teacher.

No more school, she thinks.
All she can hear is an ambulance siren and guns firing.
The school stands *burning* in front of her.
Her school was bombed in front of her eyes.

She runs towards home without tears in her eyes.
However, she promises to continue dreaming.
You can destroy the whole world but you can never kill a dream.

At the Edge of Suicide
mixed media: pastels, colored pencil, acrylic on paper, acrylic on canvas
copyright by Steffi Hekli/world

At the Edge of Suicide

Standing on the edge of the terrace,
I measure the distance to the ground.
It's high enough to kill.
I see myself at the edge of falling down.
The wind pushes me, yet I stand firm.

I want my soul to fly away after I jump—
feel the breeze on my face
soaring weightless and groundless.

For the last time, I want to visualize
the times I walked on the grass,
walked on the snow while shattering with every step,
walked on the beaches
while the sun hid behind the mountain.

The type of picture without sound—just moving images.

To visualize the big smile on the face of a child
who had a loaf of bread under his armpit, rushing towards home.
I picture a fair world for all the children,
the picture where every child has enough to eat,
where money is not the enemy.

For the last time, I want to live.
The child in the picture tells me—not this time.
Then, I step back from the edge of suicide.

Mornings in Kabul
oil pastels on paper
copyright by Steffi Hekli/world

Mornings in Kabul

Our window is ragged,
yet our memories are still new.
From this side of the window, I see
our alley sitting peaceful and empty.
Ignorance has swollen the city
and its peaceful nights.
Its silence has run through everything.
Riots have become unceasing.
Mornings are scary.
Its blossoms are seared and dead.
This silence terrifies me.
These unpaved alleys terrify me.
Mornings in Kabul terrify me.
The city is waiting for an uproar to break the chain.
It is waiting for a brand new day to rise from ashes

and flowers to flourish.
The city is waiting for strength to break the pain.
It is waiting for a brand new generation
to heal every wound,
to grow every day.
A salute to you, new generation,
for you will bring peace and education.

Death Must Be So Beautiful

They said death is not the end,
that it must be so beautiful.
They said after I die
I could touch the sky,
ride the stars,
walk in the cosmos.
They said after I die, I live endlessly.
I will see the other side
where I desire to hide
from what I saw when alive.

They said death is the beginning.
That must be a mystery,
seeing ending then beginning.

When my soul leaves the earth,
bring dervishes.
Let them swing.
Ask them to sing,
for I am leaving the earth.

It must be a happy ending,
for my soul is penetrating the invisible.
They said I will be reborn so we all will reunite.
Earth wouldn't be our property.
Then death must be a spark ready to ignite.
They said there would be a judgment.
I will demand justice from those who ignored my death,
from those who served me with weapons and bullets,
from those who have had a luxurious life
yet left me whilst I needed help.

Now I know why death is so beautiful,
since I won't see others saved
while I am at risk, as if I were not part of them.

Band e Amir, Bamiyan, Afghanistan
photograph copyright by Nematullah Ahangosh

The Reality

A man who kills one man becomes a murderer.
A man who kills millions becomes a hero.
In a world where hatred substitutes for love,
the destiny shall become lightless.

O, daughters of truth,
I have seen us in the past
as an alternate reality
where we were humane and one.
O, sons of the present,
I have seen us
as a parallel reality
where we existed as a family.

O, humans so earthly,
we are meant to act wisely.
I invite us again for one reality,
an alternate and parallel creation,
for we are one heart.

A man who kills one man kills all humanity.
He who saves one, he saves all.
He who sets one man free,
he shall live easy and worthy.
You are my reality.
I am your parallel.
Together, we are our alternates,
for we are a light in our dark days.
We are all one human race.

Teach to Love
pastels, colored pencil, and paper on paper
copyright by Steffi Hekli/world

Teach to Love

I wish I could stop time,
trap the wisdom in me.
I wish I had light in hand,
no plans in head,
teach those who can't love,
love those who teach—continue to teach and to love
without command and judgment,
only love, love, and love.

I wish we didn't forget to look at the clouds
and treasure their beauty.
I wish we could play more music
and wish I could be as Rubab to humans,
animals, and to nature,
bringing good music and deeds to all.
I wish I could sing unity to youth,
to children, and to everyone.

This endless war costs us everything.
I wish we could abolish it
before it abolishes us—all.

How We Fight COVID-19 in Afghanistan

This is a message.
This is a story.

I am sitting across the bed where part of me is sleeping.
Maybe she is not sleeping.
She is just pretending to keep me happy,
and I pretend that I'm happy she is recovering.
We are both terrible liars.

She raised me and trained me to be a warrior.
I am now by her side to raise her.
She lost muscles and hope.
But she did not lose me.
She knows that and still loses hope.
I know the same.
We are terrible fighters.

Mom, you have been my teacher
without a degree and without charging a fee,
but the doctors charged us more than what a teacher does.
You never told that part of the story.
Perhaps it has never been part of it,
and the doctors and the private hospital did not appear anywhere.
This is the reason we brought you home.
I, too, weep when the room is the dark of nights.
I am an awful learner.

I know we could afford the hospital,
but there is one lesson the doctors taught me—that
never crossed our minds—that corruption fuels the doctors' pockets,
not the health—
where the money replaces ethics,
where patients are not the priority.
We need to fight the virus alone but together,
away from the corruption, close to each other.

The hard part is that I can't move myself better.
How could I help you, Mother?
I am not sure whether to thank or to hate others for this.
I am just watching you being helped—not by me.
That really hurts, Mom,
not inasmuch as I'm disabled.
I have never seen such a love—
not in scriptures,
not in any religion, and certainly not in any book.
What a border-free religion we believe in.
What a beautiful prophecy and
what a story of bravery we are writing.
Because, Mom! Our government is worse than COVID-19,
when it can't control a private hospital.

The Drone and the Butterfly

My word is not showering like a bullet.
It does not tear like a sword.
My word is falling like rain.
It heals body and brain.

My word is not flying like a drone.
It does not kill sinful souls.
My word is soaring like a butterfly.
It is flying again and again and again.
My word connects the dots.
It comes from my heart.
My word chases the light
in the middle of nowhere.
It sings like a bird.
My word heals.
It is simple and frugal.

My word is a smile
seen on a child's face.
It comes from a mother's mouth.
My word is not a dirty smokestack.
It is like the blue sky.
My word is like a cloud
fleecy and fluffy and soft.
My word is like a song
sung by many,
understood by some,
practiced by few,
felt by all.

My word is nothing at all, yet
it is peace.

Nostalgic Sunrise in the Gazni Province
photograph courtesy of Nematullah Ahangosh

Missing Home

Sometimes I want to walk aimlessly.
Sometimes I want to disappear,
disappear into nowhere,
feel the sun on my face,
stare towards the heavens at midnight,
wander in the morning when all are asleep,
stare at the sunset
when Allah watches me beneath the heavens
as he watches how my *Allahu Akbar* is different from theirs.

Sometimes I want to go back in the past.
I wish I could reinvent the moments of
being with my family beneath a tree
to drink a cup of green tea,
to laugh endlessly,
spread the love,
share the melancholy while
sitting around a campfire and
burning hatred in it,
growing love the next morning.
Sometimes I simply miss home.

One More Time

Here and there,
out and about,
I'm wandering,
waiting for the day to come
one more time when I overcome
all challenges that war brought—
one more time:

one more cup of green tea
with a friend under a tree,
one more time to feel the sun
on my face for as long as I can,
one more time to sit in the garden
to listen to the songbird singing from heaven—
to read one more good book.

Most of all, I want to sleep
with peace of mind
without thinking about 9/11
and what it brought—

One more time
without war and fighting,
one more time
let the kids play,
fly their kites
soaring high in the sky.
Let the children laugh
a laughter that can reach heaven.
Let them to go to school without fear
one more time.
Let the mothers not worry
about their kids

just one more time.

Afghan Peace Volunteers and the Invaders

There is me.
There is you.
They are there, too.
They seek the right path
and walk around it, not on it.
Yet, we walk the right path
that is all the difference we have.
Our smiles are strong.
Their rifles are not.

They fight and fight,
yet we listen, understand,
trust, and support one another.
They fly drones.
They throw bombs.
We fly kites. We grow love.
We try to live in peace.
We are fewer in numbers,
but we're together.
They are a crowd
making noise.

We raise our voices.
We are not silent about our opposition to war.
We make our presence our resistance.
They call us mad.
Yes, we are. Let us be. We are the Afghan Peace Volunteers,
but not the way they are.
They make the borders
and invade cities.
We break their borders.
We can open all borders with love,
as in love there is no border.

Mother of All Bombs

I send you my smiles.
You send rifles across miles.
Don't send me a rifle
when you could send a pen.
See how I will try to gain
something from what's left of this game
reminding you of the pain.
Come see me again and again.
The guns you send are in vain.

Don't drop the Mother of All Bombs.
My mother is beautiful and calm.
Most mothers are kind.
She raised me.
A bomb with her name is no joke.
Her name is the name of peace.

Remember, you and I are a small piece!
Guns are not the answer.
Bombs are illusive.
Love is how we should seek peace.

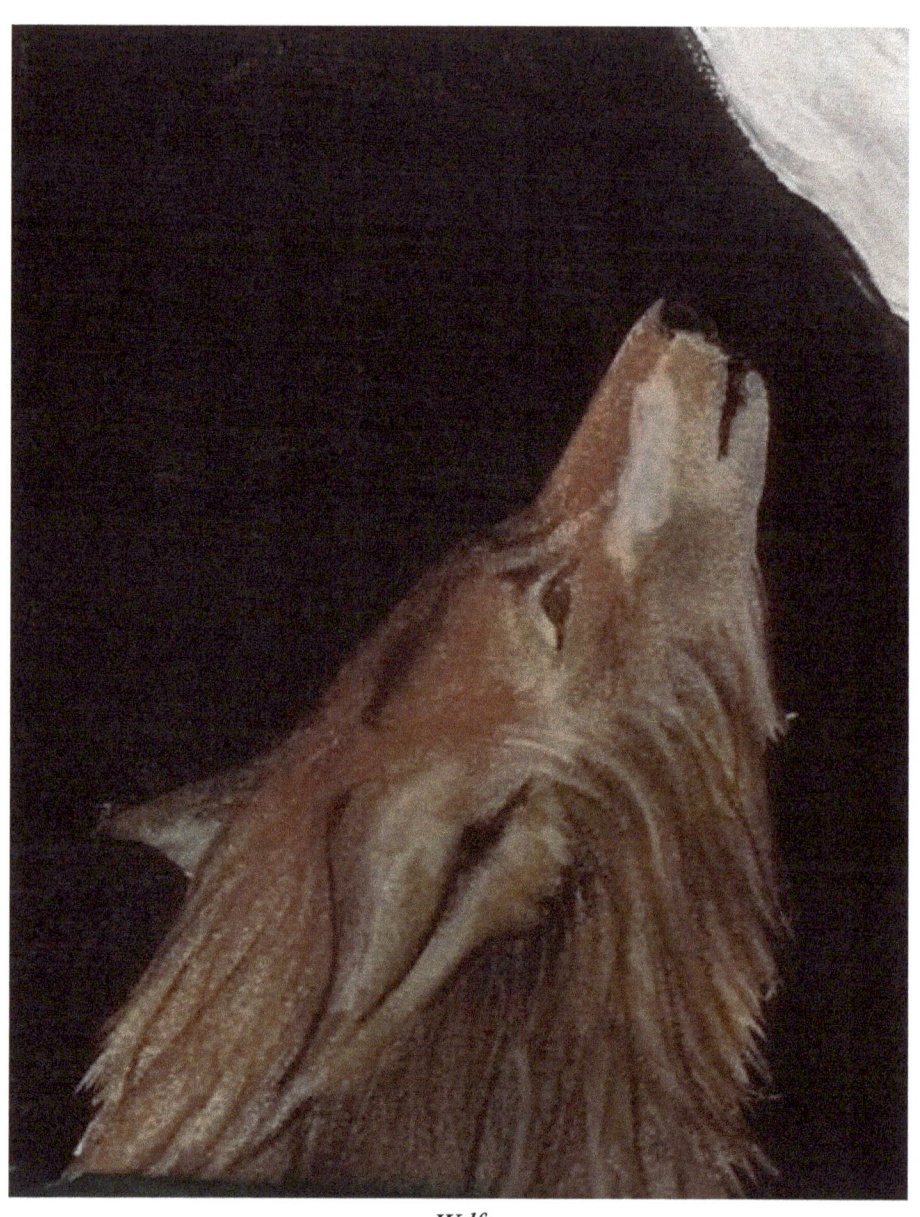

Wolf
pastels on paper
copyright by Steffi Hekli/world

The Question

There is a question.
Don't worry. I want no answer.
For a minute, I ask you to think—
but think, not answer.
The question has no answer.

If you don't trust me,
ask others this same question.
The question seeks no answer.
How can there be an answer?
When a question is not asked,
we must ask the question more,
yet answer once and only once.
This question is not easy to ask,
as there is not an answer.

A question without an answer
has always been difficult.
I urge, answer not.
This question seeks thought.
The question should lead,
lead us to think—
think to lead a life,
a life that belongs to all.

The question is:
Can we be like animals, and
not hurt our species?
They may teach us how to be humans.

Davis with Visions

Skinny like me,
he walked like Bob Marley,
right up to me –
his tuneful accent of India,
mine of Afghanistan –
to say my wallet was hanging from my back pocket.
I was agitated.

Davis Panna and Nematullah Ahangosh at their college in Chennai, India
photograph copyright by Sharon Bianca Michael

He reminded me of someone—who?—
with his worn jeans and T-shirt,
short hair,
and tattoo of an electrocardiogram on his neck.
"Thanks," I said.
Introductions exchanged as
our friendship began.
Conversations around campus—
how like-minded we were.
He was gifted at description,
sound waves flowing from his mouth
as he talked
from the Himalayas and the Amazon rainforest.
Davis connected saints and shamans.
I linked Balkh to Tabriz,
the dervishes to disciples.
Sometimes psychedelic music freed our minds,
Bob Marley singing in the background.
"Have no fear for atomic energy,
'cause none of them can stop the time . . . "
Wordless talks hiding in the smokes we shared,
our psychedelic trips brought light from former generations' spirits.
In hallucination, figures of our ancestors appeared
grateful for our friendship,
we who appreciated our existence,
our indigo auras coupling us with the old souls.
Meditate, be high or sober,
our visions and spirits enjoyed
telepathic encounters of cathartic experience.
We let go of the rest,
no scar or trauma left.

Grounded and Groundless
pastels on paper
copyright by Steffi Hekli/world

Grounded and Groundless

O, earthly! Why are we groundless?
Did we forget our elements of
love and kindness,
music and happiness,
passion and benevolence?

In spite of all, we search in black holes.
We hurt each other like pain-in-butt holes,
run after one another,
run away from each other.

One day, we'll vanish like flocks of birds.
Human rendezvous is unknown.
Even our inception is unknown.
Where we are headed is uncertainty.

We are full of ground,
yet we have never been so groundless.

We forget our very mission,
to love each other in every occasion.

Traveler and Companion

In travel companion, in life compassion.
—Haruki Murakami

Compassion is the wine of soul.
The more you taste it, the more it's ecstatic.
Dance in tune with the high frequency vibrations.
Ride a fine wave like a spiral into the infinite beauty of compassion.
The senses are wide open, inviting new perceptions.

Borders bound me to priceless flesh and bone
while I travel across the edges of the universe.
I know no companion Murakami writes of,
for I'm the traveler and the companion.
I need compassion where he says lies the treasure.

Next Time on Earth

The second time on earth,
I'll live different from birth,
will sharpen my ears to make sure
every music is heard.
Next time on earth, I will laugh
so hard until I cough.
I will gladly make it half
and share life with friends I cherish
and those whom I love.

The Childish Me

One more time, I'd like to piss
from a bridge down,
down to reach rocks never seen in water
or no one pissed on for thousands of years—
once more to walk down the road and
piss wherever I wish. Not to worry.
Just to be the difficult kid I used to be.

I don't forget the joy of pissing—
of a pissing match with my brother,
either drawing on a wall or far enough to reach our shadows in the
late afternoons.

Maybe I don't sound polite here,
but love is imperfect in its every manner.
I love the childish me.

Sometimes I simply miss my brother of my age.
With him, I have many stories to share.
One is when we lived together
while we had no idea what war meant.
Sometimes I miss my brother and the peaceful neighborhood
where Mr. Ahmad was taking his daughter every day to school
on his big bicycle with big smiles drawn on their faces.

Eight Hours

It was brief as dream.
I watched her for eight hours, secretly.
My assumption stopped me from approaching her.
What if she didn't want a war-stricken lover?
Then I let her go,
counted her every step until she faded away.

What Price Did Abdul Samad Amiri Pay?

The moon was glittering
in the alone but not lonely sky.
The world hung in the air,
and she was utterly weeping in the dark
as if it were their last night.
Her husband was sound asleep,
their daughter breathing like a kitten in between.
She was staring at the ceiling
and thinking about her husband's trip.
She loved him like a second self.

Waking up in their hushed home the next morning,
they prepared him for his voyage,
a journey none knew the end.

Leaving, he kissed his daughter on the cheeks,
saying goodbye. He hugged his wife, smelling her aura,
unaware he was smelling her for the very last time.

He boarded a cab
and started his endless journey.
They drove for hours,
stopped a little here and a little there,
the wild wind from the open side window lashing his face
like the whips landing on a horse's flanks.
As the journey continued,
abruptly the car froze
and the wind died.

Two men holding a pair of AK-47s stood before the car
saying nothing but pointing their rifles at them.

Another gunman opened the side door aggressively
and chased them all out.
The three had their faces masked.

The sun was trying to hide behind the mountains.
The shadows of the gunmen plotted bigger than themselves.
That was the last thing Abdul Samad Amiri remembered.
A stock came down on his head.

Opening his eyes, he found himself chained to a tree trunk
in an unknown space.
He then realized that he was kidnapped.
They tortured him
until one fine September morning, he was found shot several times
in the chest.
He died as a human rights commissioner.
What a price he paid.

Darulaman Palace
photograph copyright by Hakim Young

Hope in the Dark Night

On Sunday morning, I woke up as the twilight
illuminated the verges of the sky.
I told my mom I would like to order on Amazon.
She frowned and said, "No Amazon is here."
Convinced, I wondered where I learned about Amazon.
Oh, I remember.
It was in a movie I watched last night.

Monday was gone followed by Tuesday, me
thinking what else we lacked:
Alibaba and eBay.

The next morning, I woke up
with the idea of freelancing
with my DSLR in hand.
Subjects in mind, I headed out
to capture the beauty of nature and post them online
and make a career out of it.
Yet I came back empty handed.

"There is no chance of PayPal," some said.

My daydreaming cut short.

I found what we lacked.
We were left behind.
It would take us a million years to level up.
I asked the stars a way forward.
No answer but just winking.
Even if they did answer, it would
reach me after I was dead.

As I stared blankly and long at the sky,
my head began spinning.
I hardly kept my eyes open
and my mind functioning.
Understanding, a number of stars appeared and,
in the left side of the moon, shaped an H.
The rest piled up as P and E after the bright moon.
Yes. The dark night for once gave me hope.

Gods Must Have Cursed Earth

Let me begin with Pandemic Capitalism.
We had much food until yesterday,
yet we eat much less today.
Disease is publicized, yet response is privatized.
Now is the turn to talk about weapons.
We invented machines to kill.
We then justify fight with more machines.
Drones fly but carry no humans.
They call it "an eye in the sky."
They named the bombs as father and mother.
Guns are supposed to bring peace.
What a strange peace.
Come and see politics!
Gods' religions are used as tools of politics.
They must have cursed us.
Let's not forget about the media.
They rewrite the right.
They cover the uncovered
and right the wrong.
All brought us to a cul-de-sac.
It is not very late,
so let's come to common terms
and play no more games.

Our Atomic Life

We killed and killed.
We animated hate and blood.
All we invented were weapons.
I don't fear atomic bombs.
I fear the way you kill me.
I fear the way you kill you.
I fear the way you kill us.

I fear the way I stand up.
I fear when I get up and fight back.
I don't fear atomic bombs.
I fear the way I kill you.
I fear the way I kill me.
I fear the way I kill us.

That is our story today.
That was our story yesterday.
I hate this story every day
that kills our loved ones.
I hate this hatred
that makes us cry and separate.
I hate our atomic life.

I love how we forgive,
the way we give,
smiles on our faces
that remove every mess.
Let's make it a story,
a story of glory
for our history—
story of love and smiles
beyond the borders
and across the miles.

Either We Are All Terrorists or No One Is

Tanks approached
accompanying white men,
tall men, strong men
looking at us,
staring at us—the children.
I was shocked to see those humans.
I asked my father who they were.
He said they were soldiers.
They were not humans like my father,
tall father, strong father,
yet kind father.

Peasants approached.
Those men were familiar,
guns hanging on shoulders.
Their faces looked like my father's—
tall fathers, strong fathers,
not kind fathers.
I asked my father who they were.
He said they were terrorists.

I asked my father who a terrorist was.
He said he was and I was,
but I had no gun.
I was not tall, certainly not strong, and I had no tank.
I asked my father who we were.
He said we were the white soldiers.
He said we were the peasants.

Confused, I asked again who the white soldiers were.
I asked who the peasants were
and who the terrorists were.
He said they were humans,
tall humans,
strong humans.

Dance or Weapon?

In our village came dancers.
Everyone watched
with mouths open.
High but harmless,
drunk yet smiling,
the dancers opened hearts,

saying "Hi" and "Hi,"
moving here and there,
saying "Dance" and "Dance,"
singing "Love" and "Love."

In our village came soldiers.
The kids watched,
some terrified,
some excited.

In our village came dervishes
swinging and amazing,
chanting here and there.

In our village arrived soldiers
marching and shouting,
lieutenant saying "Fire" and "Fire,"
running every now and then,
killing women and children.

In our village drones flew,
bombing here and there,
watching women and children,
shooting evils and the good.

Drones were flying, bullets speeding,
and mortars exploding,
yet dervishes were swinging,
dancers dancing.
women running,
men firing,
kids crying.
Everyone and everything destroyed.
This is a warning—
our beautiful pale-blue-dot village is facing extinction.

Dance or Weapon?
pastels on paper
copyright by Steffi Hekli/world

Colorless Peace

I had a color for peace.
They changed it—to red.
It is not my color for peace.
My color for peace was blue,
blue like the sky.
Oh, no. They changed sky's color.
They made that red, too,
by flying drones.

I chose green as tree color.
They even shot the tree.
My sky is not safe.
The tree is not alive.
They kept changing,
and I kept choosing more and more colors.

Now I have no color for peace.
I have a colorless peace
like the water
flowing in the sea,
in the ocean,
no border around me.

I don't invite you to be like me,
colorless and boundless,
colorless as water,
boundless as an ocean.
Yet peace needs to be colorful.
For me peace has become colorless.
I'm not accepted by you
in my own home,
in the prison,
on my courtyard and street—
In your place, too.

This makes life colorless.
However, I am pleading to the world.
Mothers need colors.
I am pleading to my generation.
Let us make the world colorful.
Abolish the weapons.
Feel the love.
Keep humanity.
Spread friendship.
Because they are our colors.
If not, then a colorless and boundless ocean storms.

Hakim Young and Nematullah Ahangosh
photograph courtesy of Nematullah Ahangosh

Hakim

I have a friend named Hakim.
It means *healer*.
He is a mysterious man.
He knows what is right.
He has many stories to tell.

His own story began with light.
Light was his guide.
He saw light his very first moment.
In Singapore, all he could see were lights.
He knew nothing better than lights.
His story twisted when he saw light in the eyes of Afghans—
two very different places but the same light.
Most of his words have feathers that
fly from his mouth and land in hearts,
but not all of his words touch hearts.
He talks nonviolence.
He says we humans need one another.
He says he could end all wars and violence.
But people are used to war.
They can't imagine a world without it.
They call him crazy.
Maybe we should all become a little crazy to understand.
He talks beyond reality, uses his imagination,
says he would build an equal world,
says he would build a green, happy, world.
His behavior is abnormal to most people.
His laughter can be heard a mile away.
He is one of the happiest people in the world.
His face is a big smile.
He smiles for every photo.
Maybe if we could learn to smile like he does,
we would see what he sees in his imagination.
You can't find a wrong in him to right.
He looks perfect in a place like Afghanistan,
But he is scared like everyone else.

A Question of Questions

The crazy world
is drowned deep,
deeper than yesterday
and deeper every day.
Here's a question I'd really love to ask:
Is there a place for me to hide?
All I know from you is hatred.
All I know is you made the children fight.
One day I will change to a fighter, too,
but as a warrior of light.
Light will be my weapon.

Call me crazy, but the day will come
when children can be children,
when they can be warriors of light,
when mothers are at peace.

Is there a place for me to hide
from the sound of the artillery?
You made children cry, mothers worry,
and the planet a prison,
a jail for a free person.
My question of questions goes to humanity.
What have we done that made us separate and disparate?
Is there a place where we do not hide our humanity?

September in Trance

On a good September morning
when the sun was filling the streets with its yellow rays,
the pavement in PD13 near to Imam Ali Mosque
was filled with youth wandering into nowhere but their directions.
The very first look of her amazed me.
My mouth dropped wide open as she crossed across from me
like a butterfly flying away from a candle.
Turning around, her swollen buttocks, thick thighs, and breasts
under her dress touched me to the core,
her black eyes glancing at me,
a kind of gaze that touches you to the core.

Some like me were surprised by such appearances.
I sensed someone walking across from her made themselves wet.
When she chewed gum, you wished the movement of her red lips
would go on forever and replay over and over.

She simply was in fine clothes,
long dress kissing the ground, each time touching,
her hair covered by a fine white scarf
reaching her lower back and above her swollen buttocks,
some of it drifting beside her right eye.
Her beauty took me into a sudden trancelike situation
that started me talking to myself,
my words louder than a drunken brawl.
Ignoring people's look at me, I turned back to resume my way
and walked on the long shadows of buildings to the moving shadows
of young trees.
Tens of September mornings passed in trance
until the next day she appeared no more.
As I imagined a perfect death,

two possibilities of death lay before me,
one that kills, the other that chills—
one that burns, the other that bores.

Then, later on the bed, at the age of seventy-eight,
while my body fails to function,
when my lungs stop breathing—
in the end, when somebody touches me,
my body chills their hand.
I desire to hear my last pulses.
Someone mourns while shedding a tear,
even if they didn't mean it, and
carries me to my eternal home—grave.

The other in a battle field,
where in a losing battle a bullet burns my chest.
I fall on the ground
like a beaten hound
while thinking of my loved ones.
I produce a picture from my pocket.
I don't know whose face it would display.

Acknowledgments

I would like to express my deepest gratitude to David Smith-Ferri, whose thoughtful feedback and unwavering support were instrumental in bringing *The Color of Peace* collection to life. David not only offered insightful guidance on my work but also acted as the bridge between me and the publisher, making the journey possible.

A special thanks to Marcia Gagliardi, my publisher, for her belief in my poetry. Her willingness to take the time to consider and ultimately publish my poems means more than words can express.

I am profoundly grateful to my family, whose steadfast encouragement and love have been my foundation throughout the journey.

To the many individuals who inspired me to write—especially peace activists and dear friends who have shown me the true power of words and action—I extend my deepest thanks. A special mention to Kathy Kelly, whose tireless work for peace has been a guiding light and source of personal inspiration.

I am also deeply appreciative of the friends who contributed to *The Color of Peace* collection, including those who shared their photographs.

A heartfelt thank you to Steffi Hekli for her stunning artwork, which beautifully complements my poems and brings an added dimension to their meaning.

Last but not least, Sherri Maurin has my gratitude for being a good friend and editor when I initially started writing poetry.

Finally, to the readers of *The Color of Peace*, thank you. Your willingness to engage with my poems is the greatest honour, and I hope the words within speak to you as deeply as they have to me.

Nematullah Ahangosh, right, with his friend Davis Panna

About the Author

Nematullah Ahangosh is an Afghan activist and poet born with muscular dystrophy. Nemat's writing reflects themes of resilience, hope, and the hardships of Afghan society, often touching on the ravages of war and plight of those affected by armed conflicts.

Nemat began writing poetry in English around 2017 while working as a peace activist in Kabul, where he collaborated with organizations focused on nonviolence. His activism later extended to education. Nemat pursued higher education in India, where he earned a bachelor's degree at the Madras School of Social Work and studied with a scholarship from the Jesuit Refugee Service.

A resident of England, Nemat founded Stretch More, an initiative dedicated to empowering disabled individuals in conflict zones and disaster-prone areas. He holds a master's degree in conflict, security, and development from the University of Sussex, supported by a scholarship from Uni Ark Foundation.

Nemat's poetic talent has gained recognition. He won first prize in the 2023 Frederick Douglass Writing Competition organized by Uni Ark.

His literary influences include Arundhati Roy, Gabriel García Márquez, Rupi Kaur, and Harper Lee, whose works resonate with his advocacy for peace, justice, and social equality. Through his poetry and activism for those affected by war, Nemat sustains his powerful voice as he uses his art to inspire and empower others.

Colophon

Text and captions for *The Color of Peace* are set in Garamond Premier Pro. The font had its genesis in 1988 when Adobe senior type designer Robert Slimbach visited the Plantin-Moretus Museum in Antwerp to study their collection of Claude Garamond's metal punches and type designs. Garamond, a French punchcutter, produced a refined array of book types in the mid 1500s.

While fine-tuning Adobe Garamond, released in 1989, as a useful design suited to modern publishing, Slimbach started planning an entirely new interpretation of Garamond's designs based on the large range of unique sizes he had seen at the Plantin-Moretus and on the comparable italics cut by Robert Granjon, Garamond's contemporary.

Titles are set in Acumin Variable Concept. Although Acumin is based squarely on the neo-grotesque tradition, which has been one of the dominant styles in typography for more than a century, the font represents an original design, a fresh approach to the tradition. It is not a variation or an interpretation, nor is it a reply to any existing neo-grotesque typeface. It's Slimbach's own take on the neo-grotesque category. Acumin brings a subtle humanity to the architectural and modular form of the neo-grotesque.